UNBREAKABLE: HOW TO STAY MOTIVATED IN A DEMOTIVATING CORPORATE WORLD

GANESH KUMAR GUPTA

Copyright © GANESH KUMAR GUPTA
All Rights Reserved.

This book has been self-published with all reasonable efforts taken to make the material error-free by the author. No part of this book shall be used, reproduced in any manner whatsoever without written permission from the author, except in the case of brief quotations embodied in critical articles and reviews.

The Author of this book is solely responsible and liable for its content including but not limited to the views, representations, descriptions, statements, information, opinions and references ["Content"]. The Content of this book shall not constitute or be construed or deemed to reflect the opinion or expression of the Publisher or Editor. Neither the Publisher nor Editor endorse or approve the Content of this book or guarantee the reliability, accuracy or completeness of the Content published herein and do not make any representations or warranties of any kind, express or implied, including but not limited to the implied warranties of merchantability, fitness for a particular purpose. The Publisher and Editor shall not be liable whatsoever for any errors, omissions, whether such errors or omissions result from negligence, accident, or any other cause or claims for loss or damages of any kind, including without limitation, indirect or consequential loss or damage arising out of use, inability to use, or about the reliability, accuracy or sufficiency of the information contained in this book.

Made with ♥ on the Notion Press Platform
www.notionpress.com

A Letter from One Fighter to Another

Dear Reader,

If you're reading this, it means you made it to the end—not just of this book, but through countless silent battles that no one applauded.

I want to tell you this: I see you. I respect you. I stand with you.

I know what it feels like to be overlooked, underappreciated, and misunderstood. I know how heavy it is to carry silent disappointment while smiling at meetings.

But you kept going. You showed up. You endured. You've already done more than most people will ever realize.

You don't need anyone's permission to feel proud of yourself.

Keep walking your path. Keep choosing integrity, growth, and inner peace—even if nobody notices.

Because real strength isn't loud. It's quiet. It's steady. It's unbreakable.

With resilience and respect,

Ganesh Kumar Gupta

Contents

I
Introduction

Introduction: When the Dream Turns Heavy

We grow up believing corporate life is the ultimate dream. Good salary. Prestige. A routine. An identity. In 2018, I believed the same. I had just entered the corporate world with hope in my heart and stars in my eyes. I thought, "This is it. This is what success looks like." But that illusion didn't last long.

Corporate life is seductive at first. You wear good clothes, get a desk, feel respected. But slowly, it starts changing you. The respect becomes conditional. Your time is no longer yours. You miss family functions, skip sleep, lose peace of mind—just to meet a deadline or impress a boss who might not even remember your name next year.

It didn't happen overnight. It was gradual. Like boiling a frog in water. I didn't realize how deeply I was sinking until I started feeling broken—mentally, emotionally, and physically. I couldn't give time to my wife. I ignored my parents. I thought, "If I just work harder, I'll get promoted. Then I'll be happy." But that moment never came.

Instead, I saw others—often less deserving—get the promotions. I saw friends turn into competitors. I experienced backstabbing, favoritism, and gossip. Slowly, I stopped trusting people. I became anxious. Demotivated. Trapped.

There was a time I wanted to quit everything. Start a business. Go back to studying. But I didn't. Not because I didn't want to—but because I couldn't. I felt stuck. That's when I hit my lowest point. And that's when something inside me shifted.

This book is not about revenge. It's not even about success. It's about survival. It's about staying sane, strong, and self-respecting in a world that constantly tries to shrink you. I wrote this book for every employee who feels unheard, undervalued, and unseen. I wrote it because no HR manual or manager ever teaches you how to stay motivated when you feel like giving up.

Here, I'll share my story—raw, unfiltered. I'll also share what saved me: neuroscience, habits, reflection, and most importantly, **self-acceptance**. If you've ever felt like you're not good enough, this book is for you. If you're tired of pretending to be okay, this book is for you.

You are not alone. And you are not broken.

You are unbreakable.

II

The Illusion of Success

Part 1: The Dream That Sold Us All

I still remember my first day in the corporate world. It was early 2018. I walked into the office wearing my best shirt, holding onto the belief that I had finally *"made it."* The AC was cold, the office smelled of fresh paint, and the glass doors looked expensive. Everyone seemed important. Everyone looked confident. And I thought to myself, *"I want to become like them."*

That day, I felt proud. I had a job. I had a future. I had entered a world that most people dream of. My parents were happy. My friends respected me. My LinkedIn post got dozens of likes. What I didn't realize was that I had just entered a game that nobody teaches you how to play.

Corporate life sells you a dream: **respect, money, promotions, leadership.** But it doesn't tell you about the cost. You don't see the anxiety, the long hours, the fake smiles, the endless meetings, or the sleepless nights. You don't hear about the office politics, favoritism, and silent suffering behind closed cabins. All you see is the surface. *And that's where the illusion begins.*

Part 2: Chasing Shadows

In the beginning, everything feels new and exciting. You want to prove yourself. You arrive early, leave late, take ownership, and say yes to every task—even if it's not your job. You believe that if you just give your best, recognition will follow. But slowly, reality begins to crack the dream.

You start noticing things. A colleague who hardly worked got promoted because of his connections. A manager who never delivered results still got praised because he *"spoke well"* in meetings. A teammate who flattered the boss got the best projects. And you? You kept working hard, hoping someone would notice.

The truth is: **merit doesn't always win** in corporate life. Visibility, perception, and alignment with the right people matter more. You can be the most efficient person on the floor—but if you're invisible to decision-makers, it won't matter. And this realization hits you like a punch in the gut. *You feel betrayed—not by people, but by the system itself.*

Part 3: The Trap of Comparison

One of the most dangerous traps in corporate life is comparison. You start comparing your progress with your peers. You wonder, *"Why did they get promoted and not me?"* You compare salaries, job titles, perks, and even seating arrangements. Every time someone else succeeds, you feel smaller. Every time someone gets praised, you question your worth.

But what you don't see is their journey. Maybe they had contacts. Maybe they had fewer responsibilities at home. Maybe they're just better at playing the corporate game.

Whatever the reason—**comparison kills your motivation.** You stop enjoying your own growth. You stop acknowledging your effort. All you see is what you don't have. And that's how corporate life begins to take from you—not just your time or energy, but your *peace of mind.*

Part 4: Running but Going Nowhere

The corporate treadmill is real. Every day feels the same. You wake up, rush to work, attend calls, send emails, deal with drama, wait for lunch, wait for the end of day—and then do it all over again. Weekends? Often ruined by late-night emails or unfinished reports. Vacations? Postponed for *"important deadlines."* Personal life? Sacrificed for *"company goals."*

You tell yourself it's temporary. You think, *"Once I get promoted, it'll be better."* But here's the truth: that moment keeps moving. You reach one milestone, and there's another one waiting. More pressure. More responsibilities. Less time. **Less you.**

It's like running on a treadmill. You feel tired, exhausted—but when you look around, you realize you haven't really moved forward. You're still in the same place. Just more drained than before.

Part 5: When the Shine Starts to Fade

It didn't happen in one day. The change was slow, like rust creeping over steel. One day you're excited about learning a new skill. The next, you're staring at your screen wondering, *"Why am I doing this?"*

What began as excitement slowly turned into exhaustion. You start avoiding people—not because you hate them, but because you're tired of pretending everything is okay. The fake smiles, the "How are you?" small talk, the long meetings that could've been emails—all of it starts to wear you down.

The worst part? **You begin to doubt yourself.** You wonder if you're really capable. You start thinking maybe you weren't meant for this. Maybe the others are smarter. Maybe you're the problem. This kind of self-doubt isn't just painful—it's dangerous. It eats away at your self-worth. You begin to lose confidence. And once that goes, everything else starts crumbling.

The Mental Load You Didn't Expect

Nobody tells you how heavy corporate life feels after a few years. You're not just doing your job. You're also:

- Managing your image
- Navigating politics
- Protecting your reputation
- Worrying about your future
- Carrying family responsibilities

It's not just work. It's **mental gymnastics.** And slowly, you start to feel trapped—like you're living someone else's dream. You remember why you joined in the first place: to build a better life. But now, that same dream is making you question your entire identity.

You're always "on." Always reachable. Always responsive. And somewhere in that noise, *you lose connection—with yourself.* You forget what makes you happy. You forget what rest feels like. You forget how it felt to be excited about something that wasn't related to a project or deadline.

Relationships Start to Suffer

The corporate grind doesn't just affect you—it affects everyone around you. You come home late. You miss birthdays. You skip Sunday brunch. Your partner feels ignored. Your parents feel distant. Your friends stop calling.

You want to make time. You really do. But the truth is, **you're emotionally drained.** You're present physically—but mentally checked out. Too tired to talk. Too numb to laugh. Too distracted to connect.

And slowly, you begin to isolate yourself. Not because you don't care—but because you don't have the energy to care anymore. The job that was supposed to bring you respect ends up stealing your peace. The success you imagined begins to feel like a trap. And the people who truly love you are left wondering what changed.

The Illusion of the Paycheck

Let's talk about money.

Yes, corporate life pays. Sometimes, very well. But at what cost?

You may earn more than ever before—but you also spend more: on comfort, on convenience, on coping. You buy things to feel better, not because you need them. You upgrade your lifestyle, thinking it'll fill the void. But it never does.

You realize that even though your salary increased, your happiness didn't. In fact, you feel more anxious than you did when you were earning less. That's because **money can't fix what's broken inside.**

And this is the part that breaks people quietly: you stay in a toxic job because the money feels necessary. You trade your health for a higher CTC. You say yes to 60-hour weeks because you're afraid of becoming irrelevant. That's how **the illusion keeps you locked in.**

The Corporate Loop

Here's how the loop works:

1. You get hired full of excitement.
2. You work hard, waiting for validation.
3. You get overworked, overlooked, and undervalued.
4. You lose motivation.
5. You consider quitting—but fear losing income or respect.
6. You stay, hoping things will improve.
7. Nothing changes.
8. Repeat.

Breaking that loop takes awareness. And courage. But before you can break it, you have to admit you're in it. That's the first act of strength.

Part 6: Redefining Success on Your Own Terms

So what do you do when the system doesn't reward your effort? What do you do when hard work doesn't lead to promotions, when ethics don't bring recognition, and when playing fair gets you nowhere?

The answer is: **you stop depending on the system for validation.** You redefine success. Not based on titles or ratings—but based on resilience, self-growth, and inner peace.

Your job is what you do. It is not who you are.

Success is not just climbing the corporate ladder. It's surviving without losing your soul. It's being kind in a cruel environment. It's learning, growing, and staying honest when the world rewards manipulation.

If you can still smile after being betrayed—you're successful.

If you can still believe in yourself after being overlooked—you're successful.

If you can still help others while you're hurting inside—you're successful.

That kind of success isn't printed on your payslip. *It's written in your character.*

Rebuilding from Within

Once I stopped tying my self-worth to external recognition, everything changed. I began journaling daily—writing down what I learned, what I felt, and what I feared. I took 30-minute walks every morning with no phone—just me and my thoughts. I read books about neuroscience and motivation. I spoke with people outside my industry—creatives, teachers, doctors—and gained perspective.

The more I reconnected with myself, the more I realized: **I was not broken. I was just misaligned.** I had spent years trying to fit into a mold that was never made for me. And no wonder I felt so small—it wasn't a reflection of my value. It was the result of a poor fit.

That realization didn't fix everything overnight. But it gave me power. It gave me control. *And that control is everything.*

The Shift from Outcome to Effort

The biggest mental shift I made was this:

"I can't always control the outcome, but I can always control my effort."

That became my mantra. I stopped obsessing over promotions and started focusing on learning. I stopped worrying about office gossip and started building mental boundaries. I stopped waiting for others to validate me and started validating myself.

That's when true freedom began—not external freedom, but inner freedom. And once you get a taste of that, *you stop fearing the system.* Because you know: even if they don't see you—**you still see you.**

Key Truths to Remember

Let me leave you with some truths that helped me survive the illusion:

1. **Recognition is a bonus, not a guarantee.**
   Do your best—but don't expect applause every time.
2. **Not all growth is visible.**
   Mental strength, patience, emotional maturity—they don't show on charts, but they're worth more than awards.

3. **Corporate ladders are unstable.**
    Today you're up, tomorrow you might be down. Tie your identity to your values, not your position.

4. **Not every workplace deserves your loyalty.**
    Stay where you're respected. Leave when your dignity is at risk.

5. **Success should feel right—not just look right.**
    If you have peace, purpose, and progress—you're already winning.

III

Stories of Setback

Part 1: The Promotion That Never Came

I remember the day like it was tattooed on my mind. It was the end of the financial year. The office buzzed with nervous excitement. Everyone was refreshing their inboxes, waiting for appraisal results. I had every reason to feel confident—six months of nonstop weekends, covering two people's responsibilities, and delivering a high-stakes project that even senior leadership had praised. My manager had applauded me in meetings. Teammates whispered, *"This year is yours."*

And I believed them.

All day, I checked my inbox like it held the key to my self-worth. At 6:12 PM, the email finally arrived. I opened the PDF. My eyes scanned the list.

My name wasn't there.

I double-checked. Then again. Still missing. Someone else had been promoted—someone whose contribution was minimal, someone who had left early more often than stayed late. But he had something I didn't: a rapport with upper management. Casual coffees, inside jokes, shared hometowns—things that didn't show up on performance sheets but made all the difference.

I didn't cry. I didn't scream. I just... shut down.

That night I lay awake, staring at the ceiling, drowning in a flood of quiet rage and self-doubt.

"Wasn't I good enough?"

"Did I imagine all the appreciation?"

"Was it all a waste?"

It felt like betrayal—not just by a person, but by an entire system I had trusted.

Part 2: The Emotional Crash

In the weeks that followed, I was not myself. Or maybe I was—just stripped down to a raw, hurting version I hadn't met before. The ambition that once lit my mornings dimmed. I began dragging myself to work, participating in meetings like a shadow. I smiled out of habit, not happiness. The spark I had carried, that eagerness to contribute and add value—it vanished.

I started avoiding people. Especially the ones who had been promoted. It wasn't envy, exactly—it was shame. I felt like I had failed in a race I didn't even realize was rigged.

The worst part? No one noticed.

No manager checked in. No colleague asked why I'd gone quiet. In the buzzing world of deliverables and KPIs, no one had time for emotional bruises. I considered resigning. Walking away. Leaving everything behind.

But I didn't.

Not because I didn't want to—but because fear held me tighter than courage. Fear of financial instability. Fear of being judged. Fear that maybe this was all I deserved. So I stayed. Physically present. Emotionally absent. A shell of someone who once cared.

Part 3: The Turning Point

It happened on a random Tuesday.

I was staring blankly at my laptop, pretending to review a report I had already read three times. The office noise blurred into background static. That's when a senior colleague—someone I'd barely exchanged words with—walked by, paused, and asked gently, *"You okay?"*

Reflexively, I nodded.

But he didn't buy it. He sat beside me, looked straight into my eyes, and said, *"You know... promotions feel good. But clarity is better. If you're clear about who you are and what you offer, you stop needing people to validate it."*

That single sentence struck deeper than any feedback I'd ever received.

That night, I dusted off my old journal. I wrote down everything I had been holding in—the anger, the disappointment, the hopelessness. But I also wrote something new:

"Maybe the world doesn't owe me a title. But I owe myself peace. I owe myself a rebuild."

That was the beginning of something—maybe not a comeback, but a reckoning. And sometimes, that's the only place healing begins.

Part 4: Lessons from the Fall

Failure—especially unacknowledged failure—teaches you in ways success never can. That missed promotion broke me, but it also rebuilt me. Here's what it taught me, and what I hope it teaches you too:

1. **Hard Work Isn't Always Equal to Reward**
   We're told since childhood that if we work hard, we'll be recognized. That's not always true in the corporate world. Sometimes, you can be exceptional—and still be invisible. That doesn't mean stop trying. It means start choosing *why* you're trying.

2. **You Are Not the System's Shortcomings**
   Getting passed over doesn't mean you're not worthy. Sometimes, the process is flawed. Sometimes, decisions are driven by politics, not performance. Learn to separate your identity from outcomes you can't control.

3. **Pain Illuminates Priorities**
   Disappointment forces clarity. It shows you who you trust. What you value. What you need to let go of. It's painful—but it also purifies.

4. **Your 'Why' Must Be Deeper Than Recognition**
   If your only reason to excel is to be rewarded, you'll burn out. Build an internal compass—growth, integrity, learning—that doesn't depend on applause.

5. **Healing Is Nonlinear**
   There's no fixed timeline to "get over it." Some days you'll feel fine. Others, the old bitterness will sneak back in. That's okay. Healing doesn't demand perfection. It asks for patience.

Part 5: Reframing Setbacks as Signals

One realization that truly changed me was this:

A setback is not the end—it's a signal.

Sometimes, the universe blocks paths not to punish us, but to redirect us. Maybe that promotion would have locked me further into a role I wasn't meant to stay in. Maybe I needed to break down in order to break free.

I started treating that missed promotion as a wake-up call, not a failure. I enrolled in a weekend course on emotional resilience. I started therapy. I rebuilt my routines—walks, sleep, reading. I even started mentoring someone younger in the office. That single act of helping someone else reminded me of my own value.

And slowly, the fog began to lift.

I wasn't healed completely. But I was no longer helpless.

Part 6: If You're in That Place Right Now...

Let me speak directly to you.

If you're in the middle of your own setback—if you feel unseen, unappreciated, or betrayed—I want you to remember this:

- **You are not your last evaluation.**
- **You are not defined by your designation.**
- **You are not a failure just because someone else got ahead.**

You are evolving. And evolution is painful. You may not feel strong today—but strength isn't always loud. Sometimes it looks like showing up despite the weight. Sometimes it looks like crying after work but still waking up the next day. Sometimes it looks like choosing dignity over revenge.

And that quiet resilience?

It will take you further than any title ever could.

IV

The Science of Disappointment Understanding What Happens Inside You When Things Fall Apart

Part 1: The Invisible Storm Inside You

You pour your best into something—you stay late, you give your all, and you believe in the result. Then, when the outcome comes, there's no recognition. No praise. No explanation.

It feels like a sucker punch.

But this reaction isn't just emotional—it's physiological. Disappointment changes your brain's chemistry. It floods your body with stress hormones and shifts you into survival mode.

Understanding what's happening beneath the surface is the first step toward healing.

Part 2: When Your Brain Enters Survival Mode

Disappointment activates your **amygdala**, the brain's threat center. It doesn't differentiate between emotional rejection and physical danger.

Your body reacts accordingly:

- Your heart races
- Muscles tense
- Focus narrows
- Logic fades

Cortisol surges. Your **prefrontal cortex**—the part responsible for decision-making—gets suppressed. This is why you feel foggy, reactive, overwhelmed.

You might:

· Rehash conversations

· Blame yourself

· Feel rage, sadness, or shame

This is not weakness. This is **biology**.

Part 3: The Trap of Chronic Disappointment

When setbacks become a pattern, your brain adapts—but not in a good way. You start expecting the worst. You stop hoping. You protect yourself by not trying.

This state is called **learned helplessness**.

Symptoms include:

- Numbness
- Loss of motivation
- Emotional shutdown

Left unchecked, this cycle can lead to burnout, anxiety, or depression. But awareness is power. You can interrupt the loop.

Part 4: Building Emotional Muscle—Step by Step

Your brain is not fixed—it's **plastic**. Which means it can be rewired with small, repeatable actions:

1. **Observe, Don't Absorb**

   Step back from the emotional wave. Say: "This is information. Not identity."

2. **Name the Emotion**

   Science shows that simply labeling what you feel (e.g., "I feel dismissed") calms the amygdala and brings rationality back online.

3. **Shift from "Why Me?" to "What Next?"**

   Empower yourself. The goal isn't to feel good immediately, but to stay grounded enough to move forward.

Part 5: Science-Backed Habits That Heal

To strengthen your mental resilience, build these practices into your daily life:

· **Mindful breathing** – Even 3–5 minutes reduces cortisol.

· **Journaling** – Helps unpack emotions and clarify thoughts.

· **Movement** – Physical activity processes stress hormones.

· **Sleep hygiene** – Supports emotional and cognitive recovery.

· **Digital boundaries** – Prevents emotional triggers from comparison and overload.

Also, learn to see **motivation as a skill**—not something you have or don't, but something you train.

Part 6: Your Brain Is Not Broken—It's Adaptive

Let me share a personal moment. After a high-stakes presentation, the silence from leadership felt louder than words. No thank-you. No recognition. Just... silence.

I spiraled. For two days, I felt invisible. But on day three, I paused, breathed deeply, and journaled:

"This hurt. But I learned. I contributed. I grew."

Then I took a walk, wrote down three things I was proud of, and asked a teammate for feedback.

Those were small wins. But they rewired my mind.

Over time, I stopped seeing disappointment as failure—and started seeing it as **feedback**.

So if you're reading this and feeling stuck in a loop of letdowns, remember:

· Your nervous system is doing its job—but you can train it differently

· You're not weak—you're wired

· But wiring can be changed

Your mind is not your enemy—it's your greatest tool

And now, you're learning how to use it.

V

Politics Without Losing Yourself How to Stay Ethical in a Partial and Power-Driven Corporate World

The Meritocracy Myth

If you believed that corporate life was a pure meritocracy, here's your wake-up call: it's not. Promotions don't always follow effort, skill, or results. More often, they follow perception, power plays, and proximity to decision-makers.

You'll see people rising quickly—not because they deliver extraordinary work, but because they master the subtle art of pleasing the right people. You'll see how whispers in closed rooms can carry more weight than months of hard work. It's natural, then, to question: *Do I have to play dirty to survive?*

Here's the truth: **you don't**. There's a wiser way to navigate office dynamics—one that lets you succeed **without selling your soul**.

Understanding the Power Map

Office politics isn't inherently evil—it's just human behavior unfolding within structured chaos. To survive in this environment, you need to observe keenly. And to lead within it, you must learn to understand the landscape.

Start by reading the room. Who holds informal influence? Who quietly shapes decisions? What behaviors are rewarded—and which are dismissed? Think of your workplace as a **political map**, not just an organizational chart. Once you recognize the hidden lanes of power, you can navigate more intelligently.

For instance, when my team was restructured, a soft-spoken analyst—not a senior manager—suddenly began shaping key meetings. I noticed his growing influence and brought him into earlier strategy conversations. Not to manipulate, but to respect the true center of gravity. **That's what smart, ethical politics looks like.**

Building a Circle of Integrity

Choosing not to play dirty can feel lonely at first. That's why you need a **circle of integrity**—a group of people who remind you that ambition and ethics can co-exist.

Build this circle with intention. Be the kind of person others can trust—someone who keeps confidences and follows through. Offer help freely, without expecting immediate returns. And diversify your circle—connect with people across roles, functions, and even industries. These individuals become your **mirrors, anchors, and reality-checkers** in a noisy system. They help you stay rooted in who you are, even when everything else feels unstable.

Navigating Without Losing Yourself

You don't need to gossip to be relevant. You don't have to flatter to be seen. Instead, learn the art of **ethical influence**—showing up with clarity, calm, and consistent delivery.

Practice choosing silence over slander. Step away from drama with grace: *"Let's focus on solving this."* Show competence through action, not noise. And when it matters, speak up—clearly, firmly, and respectfully.

Once, a colleague was excluded from a key brainstorming session. I simply said, *"Let's hear from Priya—her input could really help."* The team benefitted, and no egos were bruised.

Another time, in a heated meeting full of blame, I offered, *"I'll take responsibility for the next steps—let's shift to solutions."* The energy in the room shifted instantly. Integrity was noticed—and respected.

Ethical politics doesn't mean absence of politics. It means conscious participation—with boundaries.

When the Environment Turns Toxic

Sometimes, the problem isn't you—it's the environment itself. When the culture becomes toxic, **you feel it in your body first**: the dread before Monday mornings, the anxiety before meetings, the ache of compromising your values repeatedly. You begin to feel like your soul is shrinking.

When this happens, seek honest input from people you trust. Define your non-negotiables. And begin quietly building your exit runway—skill by skill, connection by connection. Remind yourself: **you are not your employer. Your paycheck doesn't define your worth.** Walking away isn't weakness—it's wisdom. It's strength rooted in self-respect.

The Psychology of Power and Integrity

Social neuroscience teaches us something profound: humans are wired to detect authenticity. You don't have to chase status to build influence—**you just need to embody trust.**

When you show up with fairness, calm, and consistency, you activate trust circuits in the people around you. Over time, this builds an invisible yet powerful currency: **credibility**. And in a world full of noise, credibility is your most strategic advantage.

Final Thoughts

Office politics is like a forest. Some paths are overrun with ego, shortcuts, and shallow praise. But some trails—though quieter—are rooted in values, discipline, and clarity.

You don't have to choose between success and self-respect. You can win—**without losing yourself.**

Let others chase popularity.

You build credibility.

Because that's how real power is earned—and kept.

VI

Self-Worth Beyond Promotions

Why Your Value Is More Than Your Title

In the corporate race, it's easy to believe your value equals your title, appraisal, or pay slip. And when your self-worth gets entangled in that belief, you live in quiet anxiety—constantly chasing validation that never truly satisfies.

But here's a liberating truth:

Your real worth isn't earned through recognition—it's discovered within.

If your identity depends on a manager's nod or a yearly rating, you'll always feel unsure. True confidence comes from within—grounded in who you are, not just what you achieve.

1. Root Your Worth Internally

Self-worth built on outer validation is fragile. But when it's anchored in your inner compass, it becomes unshakable. Start with reflection.

Ask yourself:

1. What values guide my life? (e.g., honesty, kindness, curiosity)
2. How do I want people to remember me—as a teammate, friend, or human being?
3. What kind of impact do I want to create—in or outside of work?
4. When did I last stretch myself, learn something, or grow?
5. Who have I helped recently, and how?

These questions shift your lens from *"How do they see me?"* to *"Who do I choose to be?"*—and that shift builds lasting self-worth.

2. Reframe Setbacks as Feedback

When your self-worth is internal, disappointments lose their sting.

A missed promotion isn't a reflection of your potential—it's information.

Tell yourself:

- *"I gave my best."*
- *"This is one moment in a long journey."*
- *"I control my response, not others' opinions."*

This approach builds **emotional resilience**. It allows you to bend without breaking.

3. Find Purpose Beyond Your Position

Your designation can change—but your purpose stays.

Ask yourself:

- Am I nurturing my family or community?
- Am I learning something new each day?
- Am I mentoring or guiding someone around me?
- Am I creating something meaningful?

When purpose drives you, fluctuations in status don't shake you.

4. Use Affirmations to Rewire Your Mind

Affirmations aren't about hype. They are about grounding yourself in truth.

Daily phrases to try:

- *"I am more than my job."*
- *"I define my worth—not others."*
- *"I bring value wherever I go."*
- *"Setbacks are temporary. My purpose endures."*

Say them out loud—in the mirror, in your car, or during your coffee break. Let them root you.

5. Psychology of Internal Self-Worth

Psychology shows us:

Self-worth based on titles or praise creates fragile self-esteem.
You become dependent on validation—and fear criticism.

But when your worth is rooted in values and growth, you're calm in success and composed in failure.

Dr. Brené Brown puts it beautifully:

"Courage, compassion, and connection create true self-worth. These are daily choices."

6. Mini Case: Anita's Shift

Anita, a senior analyst, spiraled into doubt when she received a "meets expectations" rating. Coaching helped her reconnect to her core values: learning and helping others.

She revived her weekly study circle. Her confidence returned—not through ratings, but by **living her values.**

7. Mini Case: Rahul's Reset

Rahul linked self-worth to hours worked. When his promotion didn't arrive, he doubled down—until burnout hit.

One weekend, he switched off his devices and painted with his daughter. That moment awakened him. He began focusing on connection, creativity, and balance. And for the first time, he felt **whole.**

8. My Own Shift

There was a time I longed for a promotion as proof of my worth. When it didn't happen, I broke inside.

But slowly, I built a new identity.

- I journaled about my relationships.
- I noted the lives I touched.
- I volunteered once a month.

Eventually, I realized: **my value had never lived in a designation. It lived in me.**

9. Build a Worthy Mindset

Try this:

- **Morning Check-In:** *Who do I want to be today?*
- **Evening Reflection:** *Did I live with integrity today?*
- **Monthly Reset:** *Am I growing, contributing, and connecting?*

These questions keep you aligned with your internal compass—not the corporate scoreboard.

Final Thoughts

You don't have to earn your worth. You already have it.

When you stop chasing validation and start living your truth, you become free.

Anchored in your values, purpose, and relationships—you're unshakable.

No title, rating, or rejection can take that away from you.

VII
Habits That Heal

Daily Routines to Rebuild Motivation and Inner Peace

Corporate life can slowly chip away at your energy and spirit. With time, you begin to run on autopilot, disconnected from your purpose and drained of your spark. Motivation feels distant, and peace seems like a luxury. But healing doesn't require big, dramatic changes. It starts with small, intentional habits—daily rituals that gently nurture your mind, body, and soul. These aren't just routines; they're lifelines that bring you back to yourself.

Start Your Day with Intention

The way you begin your morning shapes everything that follows. A screen-free walk—just 15 to 20 minutes outdoors without your phone—can be more powerful than you expect. The rhythm of your footsteps, the breeze, and morning light help reset your nervous system. You begin the day grounded, not rushed.

Add to this a short journaling ritual. Spend five minutes noting what you're grateful for, what you want to focus on, and how you're feeling right now. It's like tuning your inner compass before the chaos begins. Follow it with a simple affirmation—something personal, like *"I bring value—I matter"* or *"I choose presence over perfection."* These quiet declarations of self-worth build resilience, day by day.

Reflect and Recalibrate Weekly

Life can feel like a treadmill—one week blending into the next. But a short weekly reflection breaks that cycle. Pick a quiet time—maybe a Friday evening or Sunday morning—and review your week. What went well? What challenged you? What did you learn? What do you want to improve?

Instead of judging yourself by achievements alone, celebrate your efforts. Notice your growth. Let your values—not external results—guide your plans for the week ahead. If learning matters to you more than recognition, make space for learning. When your actions align with your values, motivation becomes natural.

Keep Curiosity Alive

When you stop learning, life feels dull. Curiosity is fuel—it keeps your mind alive and your spirit engaged. Each month, choose one theme to explore. It could be something simple like mindful cooking or something bold like leadership storytelling. Capture key insights in a small journal. Reflect on how these ideas change your thinking, your conversations, your decisions.

Learning reminds you that you're not stuck—you're evolving. Even when your job feels monotonous, your mind doesn't have to be.

Connect and Contribute

Isolation quietly erodes morale, while connection restores it. Look for simple ways to share your strengths—guide a colleague through a tough project, offer honest feedback, or teach a skill to someone struggling. These acts of service reinforce your sense of value, not as a role, but as a person.

Step outside your work zone occasionally. Volunteer, join a community group, or just teach a neighbor's child. Contribution rekindles purpose. Even casual chats—asking a teammate about their weekend or commenting on a friend's post—build emotional reserves that buffer daily stress.

Make Space for Rest and Recovery

Without recovery, no amount of hustle is sustainable. Prioritize 7–8 hours of quality sleep by building a calming nighttime routine. Switch off screens an hour before bed. Dim the lights. Try light stretching or a short breathing exercise.

Before you sleep, take five minutes to reflect. What brought you joy today? What challenged you? What are you grateful for? This simple ritual settles your mind, so you drift into sleep without the weight of unfinished thoughts.

Move Daily, Even in Small Bursts

You don't need an hour at the gym to benefit from movement. Tiny, consistent moments matter—stretching every 90 minutes, correcting your posture, walking down a hallway, or even dancing for a minute during lunch. These mini-breaks refresh your body and reset your mood.

When you move, you release tension. You reconnect with your body. You return to the present.

Practice Moments of Stillness

Even a few minutes of stillness each day can transform your emotional state. Start your mornings with 3–5 minutes of deep breathing. End your evenings with a body scan, relaxing from head to toe. Have at least one mindful meal a day—no screens, just you and your food. Slowing down like this centers you. It reminds you that calm is not found—it's created, moment by moment.

My Personal Habit Journey

After a quarter where I missed every deadline and lost all motivation, I felt hollow. I wasn't just burned out—I was detached from myself. That's when I began healing, slowly.

I started with morning walks, letting nature untangle my thoughts. I journaled my fears and self-doubt. I began repeating affirmations like *"I am more than my deadlines."* I did weekly self-checks—not on performance, but on my mood and energy. I read about resilience. I helped a junior colleague without expecting anything in return. I also stopped sleeping with my phone beside me.

Three months later, the deadlines hadn't changed—but I had. I laughed again. I felt lighter. I felt alive. That's the quiet miracle of healing habits: they change your experience, not just your outcomes.

Design Your Own Healing Cycle

You don't need to follow a strict schedule—but here's a simple rhythm that works for many:

Morning: A 10-minute walk → 5-minute gratitude journaling → a personal affirmation → a nourishing breakfast

Midday: A movement break → a meaningful conversation → time to learn something small

Evening: 20 minutes of reflection or planning → connection with others or quiet reading → a calm, screen-free wind down

Before bed: Meditative breathing → body scan → restful sleep

These habits aren't about perfection. They're about progress. About building momentum, not pressure.

Overcoming Common Challenges

Everyone slips. Everyone forgets. That doesn't mean you've failed.

- **"I don't have time."** Start with just three minutes. Something is better than nothing.
- **"I forget."** Use phone reminders, sticky notes, or tie habits to existing routines—like journaling with your morning tea.
- **"It's boring."** Pair the habit with something you enjoy. Stretch while listening to music. Reflect while sipping coffee.
- **"I missed a day."** No guilt. Just restart. Healing isn't a straight line—it's a dance.

Healing doesn't come from doing more—it comes from doing what truly matters, consistently. Let your habits be your medicine. Let them bring you back to your grounded, joyful self—one small act at a time.

VIII

Rediscovering Yourself Beyond the Corporate Label

When Your Job Title Isn't Who You Truly Are

In the corporate world, it's easy to confuse **performance with identity**. Titles, appraisals, and LinkedIn endorsements start to feel like reflections of your self-worth. But beneath that curated version lies your **real self**—the one that existed long before job roles and quarterly goals.

If you've ever felt like you're *just going through the motions*, this chapter is for you. It's time to **peel back the label** and reconnect with the person behind the profession.

You Are Not Just a Designation

You're more than a "Manager," "Lead," or "VP." These roles describe what you *do*, not who you *are*.

- **Your curiosity.**
- **Your compassion.**
- **Your creativity.**

These cannot be captured in a resume bullet point. When you start defining yourself beyond your job, you begin to *reclaim your story.*

Your job is a role you play, not your identity. If it ends, you do not.

The Risk of Over-Identification

Many of us fall into the trap of over-identifying with work:

- We base our self-worth on promotions or bonuses
- We lose hobbies, friends, even personality in the daily grind
- We forget who we were before deadlines took over

This disconnection breeds burnout and an existential vacuum. You start wondering: *"What's left if I don't succeed here?"*

The answer? **Plenty.** But you must *remember* what truly brings you alive.

Signs You're Losing Yourself

- You feel emotionally numb despite professional "success"
- Your weekends no longer excite you
- You hesitate to talk about passions unrelated to work
- You feel guilt when you're *not being productive*

These are not weaknesses—they are *calls to realign.* You are being nudged back toward your essence.

Step Back to Reconnect

To rediscover who you are, give yourself permission to:

- **Pause**: Sit with yourself without a productivity agenda
- **Reflect**: Journal about what made you feel alive as a child or teen
- **Reconnect**: Reach out to people who knew you before your corporate role defined you
- **Explore**: Try new hobbies, travel differently, learn for fun again

Small Ways to Reclaim Yourself

You don't need a sabbatical to rediscover your identity. Try:

- **Morning rituals**: A few minutes of journaling, music, or meditation before screens
- **Weekend creative time**: Write, sketch, sing, or play—*just because*
- **Volunteer**: Engage with causes that align with your values
- **Digital detoxes**: Take breaks from LinkedIn and emails to reduce ego-comparison
- **Nature time**: Reconnect with the physical world around you

Let Passion Be Your Compass

You don't have to monetize everything you love. Not every hobby must become a side hustle. Some passions are sacred simply because they **remind you of who you are** when no one's watching.

When was the last time you did something just for the joy of it?

Start there.

Identity Isn't Static—It Evolves

Your corporate title may change. Your role might end. But *you*—your humor, your heart, your story—will remain. The more you nurture that core, the more resilient you'll become to professional storms.

Don't let the system shrink you into a version it prefers. Instead, let your life reflect the **complex, beautiful, expansive** human you are.

Final Thoughts

Taking back control isn't about rebellion—it's about *returning to your center*. It's about writing a life that reflects who you are—not who the corporate ladder wants you to be.

Let those **slow reminders**—the *small sparks*—guide you. And once you begin, the path will unfold under your feet.

IX
Creating Your Path

Designing a Career and Life That Align with Your True Self

Corporate life often feels like the default route to success—but it isn't the only one. For many, the structure becomes a cage: safe, predictable, but *deeply misaligned*. The truth is, **you're not trapped unless you choose to be**. This chapter is about stepping out of passive compliance and stepping into **intentional creation**—of a career, lifestyle, and identity that reflect your full self.

Step 1: Own Your Power to Choose

Even within rigid systems, you hold the power of choice. It may not feel dramatic or rebellious—but subtle shifts matter. You can:

- **Stay** in your role and navigate it with greater clarity and purpose
- **Pivot** toward something that lights up your mind and soul
- **Combine** both to build a hybrid life where fulfillment isn't delayed

Begin with awareness. For the next 48 hours, notice every time you feel stuck or resentful. Then, rewrite that moment—*What action could I take instead?* That's where your power quietly lives.

Step 2: Launch a Side Project or Hobby

Side projects are more than passion outlets—they are **safe experiments** for reinvention. They allow you to test, play, fail, and grow without risking your entire identity.

Explore what ignites you:

- **Writing**: A blog, memoir, or short stories

- **Business**: A product, service, or consulting gig
- **Education**: Teaching workshops, tutoring, creating online content
- **Creative arts**: Painting, photography, music, crafts

What matters is not perfection, but **participation**. These small expressions bring back your spark, **restore confidence**, and may even unlock new paths—professionally or personally.

Step 3: Evaluate a Career Switch or Entrepreneurship

If your corporate culture constantly suffocates your voice, a full pivot isn't reckless—it's reasonable. Start by assessing where you stand:

1. **Skill audit**: What are you good at, and what do you enjoy doing?
2. **Interest exploration**: What industries excite your curiosity?
3. **Low-risk experiments**: Freelance, volunteer, or take a short course
4. **Network building**: Talk to people already in roles you aspire to

Entrepreneurship and switching fields come with uncertainty—but **when chosen consciously**, they become thrilling adventures rather than midlife crises.

Step 4: Commit to Lifelong Learning

The world is changing fast—and your resilience lies in your willingness to keep learning. This doesn't require degrees or massive time investments.

- **Microlearning**: Spend 15 minutes a day on platforms like Udemy, Coursera, or blogs
- **Soft skill upgrades**: Revisit empathy, storytelling, and systems thinking
- **Broaden your mind**: Read outside your field—philosophy, science, art
- **Join communities**: Writers' groups, tech forums, social clubs—engage meaningfully

Learning isn't just about survival—it's about **staying relevant and joyful** as you evolve.

Step 5: Build a Supportive Ecosystem

You're not meant to walk this path alone. Your growth will accelerate when you're surrounded by people who believe in your vision.

Create layers of support:

- **Emotional tribe**: Friends and family who offer warmth, not judgment

- **Accountability circle**: People pursuing side projects or pivots like you
- **Informational network**: Industry professionals and mentors
- **Inspirational allies**: People who show you what's possible

Schedule regular conversations. Celebrate tiny wins. Share fears openly. *Together, the unknown becomes less intimidating.*

Step 6: Align with Identity and Purpose

You'll move faster when you know *why* you're moving at all. Purpose brings clarity to chaos, and identity anchors your actions in meaning.

Try this:

- **Value check**: Ask, *What kind of legacy would I be proud of in 10 years?*
- **Purpose prompt**: Complete the sentence, *I want to create ___ so that ___.*
- **Monthly check-in**: Revisit and revise your purpose as you grow

This alignment becomes your compass. When systems shift or roles disappear, your **inner direction** will remain steady.

Story: Shilpa's Reinvention

Shilpa was a successful finance executive—but promotions left her feeling hollow. She took up pottery, quietly, every morning before work. She never planned to leave her job, but after six months, she began selling her pieces at a local café.

One conversation led to another. Soon, she found herself interviewing for a strategy role at a creative startup—*a job that combined her financial acumen with her newfound artistic side.*

Today, Shilpa advises creative businesses on growth strategies. She didn't burn down her corporate life—she **built a new room within it**. Her side project wasn't an escape. It was a **bridge back to herself**.

Final Thoughts

Creating your path is not about escape—it's about *crafting with intention*. It's about designing a life in which your **identity, values, passions, relationships, and work** don't just coexist—they **nourish** each other.

Each small step—a new skill, a side project, a supportive conversation—does more than change your path.

It changes you.

Conclusion: You Are Bigger Than This

Rediscovering Strength Beyond Corporate Limits

Corporate life can shape you—but it does not get to define you.

You've seen favoritism, burnout, and broken morale. So have I. These systems can wear you down, but they can't take away what truly matters—**unless you surrender it.**

Here's what remains untouched by any toxic culture, bad boss, or broken structure:

- **Your values**—the core truths that guide you
- **Your resilience**—the quiet force that refuses to quit
- **Your capacity to learn and love**—which no rating can measure
- **Your right to choose**—to realign your life with meaning and joy

You are *not* a role, a rating, or a review.
You are a full, vibrant human being with stories, talents, and dreams far too large to be boxed in by a job title.

Transform Pain Into Perspective

Setbacks aren't punishments—they're signposts. When life goes off-script, it's not a failure. It's an invitation to pause, reflect, and grow. Instead of running from pain, *get curious*:

- Ask: *"What can this teach me?"*
- Reflect: *"What strengths have I discovered in this moment?"*
- Decide: *"How will I use this experience to build forward?"*

When you meet pain with honesty and intention, you transform it into clarity—and that's a superpower.

Fuel Growth with Disappointment

Failure is not an end—it's a beginning. Every disappointment you've endured has nudged you toward deeper alignment:

- It forced you to question false beliefs
- It pushed you to set new boundaries
- It made you re-learn what matters

You move from *"I failed"* to *"I evolved."* That's how wisdom is built—from broken expectations to powerful truths.

Stay Rooted in Your Core Strengths

There are three pillars that will keep you unshakable, even in chaos:

1. **Anchor in your values** – Let them guide you when systems collapse
2. **Talk honestly to yourself** – Acknowledge your emotions without shame
3. **Hold hope as a daily practice** – Because hope is not weakness. It is *strength in motion*

Even when the world doesn't see your worth, **you must never forget it**.

The Revolution Starts Within

You Are Never Alone

If you've ever felt isolated in this journey, hear this now:
You are not alone. Not for a single step.

- Thousands of people have walked through silent struggle and emerged stronger
- When we open up and share our stories, we create a *resilient community*
- By lifting others, you also lift yourself

In a world that teaches you to compete, *choose connection*. It heals more than you know.

Tap Into Your Unbreakable Motivation

Your deepest motivation won't come from promotions or praise. It will come from something **far more enduring**:

An unwavering belief in who you are, what you stand for, and what you dream of building.

That's what no manager can strip away.

That's your revolution—*quiet, powerful, internal.*

It begins not with a job change, but with a mindset shift.

A Final Reminder as You Close This Book

Let this stay with you:

- You are **not** your job
- You are **not** your salary
- You are **not** defined by someone else's opinion

You are your **values**, your **vision**, your **courage**, and your **capacity to love, learn, and lead**.

You will walk through storms, but you carry within you **a compass calibrated to something far deeper than KPIs**.

Something brighter. Something **bigger**.

Your Next Steps

1. **Reflect**: Write down one lesson your corporate journey has taught you—own it fully

2. **Act**: Take one small step that reaffirms your worth today
3. **Connect**: Reach out to someone who's navigating a similar path. Remind them—and yourself—that none of us are alone in this

Because when you start living like this:

- You don't just survive
- You don't just endure
- **You thrive—in every way that matters**

You are bigger than this. And you always have been.

www.ingramcontent.com/pod-product-compliance
Lightning Source LLC
Chambersburg PA
CBHW031248130726
47988CB00008B/3294